CHAPTER 1:
EXCUSE
DELIVERY

Welcome to "The Little Book of Tennis Excuses," where we take the art of excuse-making to new heights. In this section, we'll equip you with the skills needed to deliver tennis excuses with a straight face and a twinkle in the eye.

Let's dive into some invaluable tips for delivering tennis excuses with just the right touch of humor:

Maintain a Deadpan Expression: Picture this: you're delivering your excuse with a completely serious face, as if your explanation is the most rational thing in the world. By maintaining a deadpan expression, you'll create a delightful contrast between the seriousness of your delivery and the absurdity of the excuse itself.

Use Dramatic Pause: Before you unveil your excuse, pause for a brief moment. Let the anticipation build, and create an aura of intrigue around your explanation. This dramatic pause will heighten the comedic effect, leaving your fellow players eagerly awaiting your excuse.

Example: "You won't believe it, but just as I was about to serve, a mischievous butterfly landed on my racket and whispered, 'Try a topspin, my friend!' How could I ignore such wise counsel?"

Emphasize with Hand Gestures: Adding animated hand gestures to your storytelling can make your excuse come to life. Mimic the motions of your tennis shots, the swaying of the net, or even imaginary tennis ball trajectories to inject a playful element into your excuse.

These tips will help you deliver tennis excuses with impeccable timing and style. Get ready to turn those challenging moments on the court into opportunities for laughter and camaraderie!

INTRODUCTION

Welcome to "The Little Book of Tennis Excuses"! Whether you're a seasoned tennis pro or a newcomer to the court, we've all experienced those matches when the ball just doesn't seem to bounce your way, and frustration sets in. But don't worry, because this little book is here to provide you with a delightful collection of inventive excuses for those moments when your tennis adventures take an unexpected turn.

Tennis is a sport that demands precision, technique, and a keen understanding of the court's dynamics. However, even the most skilled players can find themselves mystified, wondering why their serves are off the mark or their volleys seem to lack finesse. It's during these moments that the art of excuse-making becomes a valuable skill.

Within the pages of this book, you'll discover over 100 unique excuses that encompass the myriad of factors that can influence your tennis performance. From weather-related challenges and equipment quirks to court conditions and distracting spectators, this book covers it all.

So, whether you're in search of a witty response to placate your tennis buddies or simply looking for a bit of humor to lighten the mood after a challenging match, "The Little Book of Tennis Excuses" is your go-to source. Let this collection of excuses remind you that, even on those days when your tennis game feels a bit off, the joy of being on the court and the anticipation of your next rally are always worth it.

So sit back, take a breather, and remember that sometimes the most entertaining part of the game is crafting the perfect excuse!

Enjoy your time on the tennis court, and may your stories of tennis mishaps and triumphs be a source of laughter and camaraderie for years to come!

Ace O'Blame

TABLE OF CONTENTS

Maintain a Twinkle in the Eye: While explaining your excuse with a serious demeanor, let your eyes twinkle with mischief and shared amusement. This subtle sparkle signals to your tennis companions that you're all in on the playful moment.

Example: "Ah, that missed shot? Well, you see, the tennis balls in these parts have developed a mischievous streak. They enjoy taking unexpected detours, much to the surprise of players like me!"

Play with Sarcasm: Infuse your excuse with a touch of sarcasm to deliver it in a tongue-in-cheek manner. Use irony to signal to your fellow tennis players that you're fully aware of the humorous nature of your explanation.

Example: "Of course, I intentionally hit the ball into the net. It's part of my top-secret strategy to keep the net from feeling lonely. Someone's got to pay it some attention!"

Employ a Touch of Irony: As you share your excuse, add a hint of irony to your tone to underscore the delightful absurdity of the situation. This dry humor will let your tennis buddies know that you're crafting an excuse with a playful wink.

Example: "I aimed for the baseline, but you see, the tennis court is a stage for unpredictable dramas. The ball decided to pursue a career in acting and dramatically rolled out."

Remember, the essence of delivering tennis excuses with a straight face and a twinkle in the eye is to blend earnestness with a playful spirit. Practice these tips, adapt them to your personal style, and revel in the laughter and camaraderie they bring to your tennis adventures!

Ace O'Blame

"You are never really playing an opponent. You are playing yourself, your own highest standards, and when you reach your limits, that is real joy."

ARTHUR ASHE

CHAPTER 2:
THE
EXCUSES:
RELATABLE

Inclement Weather: Unfavorable weather conditions like heavy rain, intense heat, strong winds, or extreme cold can greatly affect my performance on the court. For example, rain can make the court slippery, while extreme heat can lead to exhaustion.

Lack of Concentration: Factors such as excessive noise, court maintenance, or distractions from neighboring courts can disrupt my focus and hinder my gameplay. These distractions can make it difficult to concentrate on the game.

Lack of Proper Footing: If the court surface is wet, slippery, or in poor condition, it becomes challenging to maintain proper footing and execute shots effectively. This can lead to unforced errors and frustration.

Equipment Malfunction: Any issues with my tennis racket, strings, or shoes can significantly impact my ability to play at my best. For instance, a broken string can result in erratic shots.

Injury or Pain: Sudden injuries or nagging pains in various body parts, like the shoulder, knee, or back, can hamper my mobility and shot accuracy. Playing through pain can be challenging and affect performance.

Lack of Court Time: Not having enough practice or time on the court recently can result in rusty strokes and poor timing. Consistent practice is crucial for maintaining skill.

Opponent's Skill: Sometimes, the opponent simply plays exceptionally well, making it difficult for me to keep up. Facing a highly skilled opponent can be a tough challenge.

Mental Fatigue: Mental exhaustion or stress can affect my decision-making and concentration during a match. A distracted mind can lead to errors.

Poor Warm-up: Inadequate warm-up or preparation before the match can lead to slow reactions and stiff movements. A proper warm-up is essential to perform at one's best.

"Champions keep playing until they get it right."

BILLIE JEAN KING

Unfamiliar Court: Playing on an unfamiliar court surface or in an unfamiliar environment can throw off my game. Adjusting to different court conditions can take time.

Inadequate Preparation: Sometimes, I might not have had enough time to warm up properly or practice my shots before a match. This lack of preparation can lead to a slow start and unforced errors.

Change in Court Surface: Adjusting to different court surfaces like clay, grass, or hardcourt can be challenging. Each surface has its unique characteristics, and a sudden switch can disrupt my rhythm.

Opponent's Mind Games: My opponent might engage in psychological tactics, such as trash-talking or strategic timeouts, to distract me and disrupt my focus during the match.

Injury Recovery: Even if I've recovered from an injury, I might not be playing at my best due to lingering physical discomfort or fear of reinjury.

Crowd Disturbances: Unexpected noises or disturbances from the crowd, like cheering, heckling, or even mobile phones ringing, can disrupt my concentration and affect my game.

Food or Nutrition: Poorly timed meals or unfamiliar foods can lead to discomfort or a lack of energy during a match. This can impact my performance negatively.

Travel Fatigue: Frequent travel for tournaments can result in jet lag, sleep disruptions, and general fatigue, affecting my overall physical and mental state on the court.

Pressure and Expectations: High-pressure situations, such as playing in front of a large audience or facing a must-win match, can lead to nervousness and uncharacteristic errors.

Unlucky Bounces: Tennis balls can sometimes take unpredictable bounces due to court imperfections or irregularities, making it challenging to anticipate and respond effectively.

Racket String Tension: Changes in racket string tension can affect the control and feel of my shots. If the tension isn't just right, it can lead to mishits and loss of accuracy.

"Tennis is mostly mental. You win or lose the match before you even go out there."

VENUS WILLIAMS

New Tennis Balls: Some players blame the use of new tennis balls, claiming that they are too bouncy or slippery. They argue that they prefer the feel of slightly worn-in balls for better control.

Court Conditions: Complaining about the court conditions, such as uneven surfaces, cracks, or slippery spots, can be a common excuse. These conditions may disrupt a player's footwork and shot execution.

Line Calls: Questioning line calls and accusing opponents of making incorrect calls can be an excuse to express frustration. Disagreements over calls can disrupt the flow of the game.

Late Arrival: If a player arrives late due to traffic or other delays, they might use this as an excuse for not being mentally prepared or warmed up properly.

Bad Luck: At times, players attribute their losses to bad luck, like hitting the net cord at crucial moments or the ball narrowly missing the line.

Partner's Performance (Doubles): In doubles matches, players might blame their partner for not covering the court effectively or missing key shots.

Time of Day: Excuses related to the time of day are common. Some players claim they perform better in the morning or afternoon and blame their performance on playing during their less optimal time.

Opponent's Gamesmanship: Accusing an opponent of gamesmanship, such as taking excessive time between points or distracting behavior, can be a way to explain poor performance.

Psychological Pressure: The mental aspect of tennis is crucial. Some players may use psychological pressure, like stress or anxiety, as an excuse for their performance.

Unpredictable Weather: Tennis can be challenging when faced with unpredictable weather conditions, such as sudden rain showers, strong winds, or scorching heat, which can throw off your game.

"I'll let the racket do
the talking."

JOHN MCENROE

Fatigue from Previous Match: Players might blame their performance on tiredness from a previous match or practice session, claiming they didn't have enough time to recover.

Dislike for Court Surface: When playing on a different court surface than usual (e.g., switching from clay to hardcourt), some players use this as an excuse for not performing at their best due to the need to adapt to the surface.

Opponent's Intimidation: Tennis is a mental game, and some players might excuse their performance by claiming their opponent's reputation or demeanor was intimidating.

Ball Speed and Bounce: Complaining about the speed or bounce of the tennis balls used can be an excuse. Some players prefer faster or slower balls based on their playing style.

Uncooperative opponent: If my opponent is playing too well, there's not much I can do. They're just too good.

Health Issues: Players may use health issues, such as allergies, minor illnesses, or general discomfort, as an excuse for their performance.

Inadequate Warm-Up Partner: Blaming a poor warm-up partner for not providing a proper warm-up can be an excuse for sluggish play.

Negative Crowd: Some players might complain about the crowd being too loud or distracting, affecting their concentration and performance.

The pressure of the Match Situation: Excusing performance due to the pressure of a critical match or the presence of an important spectator, like a coach or family member.

Equipment Changes: Players may claim that recent changes in their equipment, such as a new racquet or shoes, are affecting their game negatively.

Opponent's Defensive Play: Sometimes, your opponent's defensive strategies can be so effective. They consistently return your shots, making it difficult to score points.

"The champion has failed
more times than the
beginner has even tried."

ANONYMOUS

Injured Wrist: Claiming an injured wrist can explain difficulties with forehands, backhands, and serves. It's a classic excuse to deflect from a lackluster performance.

Overhead Sun: Blaming the sun for poor play is common, especially when serving or hitting high balls. The sun's glare can make it challenging to see and track the ball accurately.

Heavy Racket: Complaining about using a heavy racket suggests that your equipment hindered your performance. It's a subtle way to admit that your skills are better than your gear.

Uncomfortable Shoes: Uncomfortable or ill-fitting tennis shoes can lead to blisters or discomfort during play, impacting your performance.

Tight Muscles: Stiff or tight muscles can limit your range of motion and affect your agility on the court. This excuse implies that your body wasn't in peak condition.

New Tennis Balls: Some players struggle when switching to new tennis balls, as they can behave differently from worn ones. This excuse points to the ball as the culprit.

Psychological Pressure: Blaming the pressure of the match itself is a psychological excuse. It suggests that the importance of the game affected your performance.

Wrong Shot Selection: Selecting the wrong type of shot can lead to unsuccessful plays. Picking a shot that doesn't suit the situation or your opponent's playing style can result in unforced errors.

Equipment Malfunction: Equipment can malfunction, your tennis gear, like rackets or strings, can fail during a crucial match, affecting your ability to perform at your best.

Peak Playing Seasons: Playing tennis during the peak season when courts are crowded can be challenging.

"I don't play opponents; I
play the ball."

SERENA WILLIAMS

Wind Conditions: Strong winds can affect the trajectory and speed of the ball. This excuse suggests that the wind was not in your favor.

Late-Night Match: Claiming fatigue from playing a late-night match shifts the blame to external scheduling factors.

Rusty Skills: Admitting that your skills are rusty due to lack of practice can explain a poor performance.

Nervousness: Nerves can affect anyone's game. This excuse suggests that anxiety or nervousness was a significant factor.

Bad Line Calls: One of the most common excuses is blaming bad line calls. Players might claim that their opponent was making horrible calls, which they believe affected the outcome of the match. This excuse often arises from frustration with officiating.

Opponent's Playing Style: Some tennis players make excuses about their opponent's playing style. They might say, "I can't play against pushers," referring to opponents who use a defensive strategy. This excuse is used to shift the blame for a loss onto the opponent's tactics.

Court Conditions: Players occasionally attribute their poor performance to court conditions. For example, they might claim that there was a leaf on the court that distracted them during a crucial point. This excuse involves blaming external factors for their mistakes.

Equipment Issues: Tennis players sometimes blame their equipment for a subpar performance. They might say that their strings were too tight or that they were struggling with "tennis elbow." These excuses focus on the physical aspects of the game.

Mental Distractions: Mental distractions can be a convenient excuse. Players might mention that they were distracted by various factors, such as noisy spectators or their opponent's grunting. This type of excuse shifts the focus away from their own performance.

"You've got to take the
initiative and play your game. In
a decisive set, confidence is the
difference."

CHRIS EVERT

New Technique: This is a great excuse to use if you're struggling with a particular aspect of your game, such as your serve or your backhand. It shows that you're dedicated to improving your game and that you're not afraid to experiment.

Not In The Zone: This excuse is perfect to use if you're struggling to focus or if you're just not playing your best. It's honest and it's something that even the best players experience from time to time.

Recovering From A Minor Injury: This excuse is perfect to use if you're not fully recovered from a minor injury, such as a sore muscle or a blister. It shows that you're being cautious and that you don't want to risk re-injuring yourself.

Tricky Opponent: This excuse is perfect to use if you're playing against an opponent who has a very different style of play than you're used to. It shows that you're aware of the challenges you're facing and that you're doing your best to adapt.

Simply Not Having A Good Day: This excuse is simple and straightforward, but it can be very effective. It shows that you're honest and that you're not afraid to admit when you're not playing your best.

Just Trying To Have Fun: This excuse is perfect to use if you're not taking the match too seriously or if you're just trying to enjoy yourself. It shows that you're having a positive attitude and that you're not too stressed about winning.

Trouble With My Serve: This is a classic excuse that can be used by players of all levels. It's honest and it's something that everyone experiences from time to time.

Not Hitting My Backhand Well: This is another common excuse that can be used by players of all levels. It's specific and it shows that you're aware of the area of your game that needs improvement.

"In tennis, it is not the opponent
you fear, it is the failure itself,
knowing how near you were but
just out of reach."

ANDY MURRAY

Wrong Tennis Shoes: Players might claim that their shoes were uncomfortable or not suitable for the court surface, affecting their performance.

Early Morning Matches: Morning matches can be challenging for some players, and they might use early wake-up times as an excuse for sluggish play.

Unfamiliar Tennis Balls: Players might say that they struggled because the new tennis balls used in the match didn't suit their playing style.

Tough Draw: In tournaments, players might argue that they had a tough draw, facing strong opponents early in the competition.

Pre-Match Distractions: Personal distractions or stress before a match can lead to excuses about not being mentally prepared.

Late Night: Players who had a late night or insufficient sleep may blame fatigue for their performance.

Bad Luck: Sometimes, players simply blame bad luck, ascribing their performance to unfortunate circumstances.

Lacking A-game: This is a simple excuse that can be used to explain any poor performance. It's a bit vague, but it's effective.

Bad Night's Sleep: If you're well-rested, you're more likely to have the energy and focus to play your best tennis.

I Ate Too Much: Eating a heavy meal before a match can make you feel sluggish and tired. It's best to eat a light, healthy meal that will give you energy without weighing you down.

Too Focused On My Opponent's Weaknesses: It's important to focus on your own game, not on your opponent's weaknesses. If you're too focused on your opponent, you're more likely to make mistakes.

"I play each point like my
life depends on it."

RAFAEL NADAL

Failure To Commit To Practice Time: The more you practice, the better you'll become at tennis. If you don't have enough time to practice, you're more likely to play poorly in matches.

My opponent was just playing too well: Sometimes, you just have to give credit to your opponent. If they're playing their best tennis, there's not much you can do.

I made a few bad mistakes: Everyone makes mistakes, but they can be especially costly in tennis. If you make a few bad mistakes, it can ruin your chances of winning a match.

I was unlucky with a few line calls: Close line calls can be frustrating, especially if they go against you. However, it's important to remember that the linespeople are doing their best and that bad line calls are a part of the game.

I was too busy thinking about my next match: It's important to stay focused on the current match, but sometimes it's difficult to avoid thinking about your next match. If you're thinking about your next match, you're more likely to make mistakes in the current match.

The wind was blowing the ball all over the place: This excuse is also a good one to use on a windy day. It can be difficult to control your shots when the wind is blowing hard, especially if you're not used to playing in those conditions.

The court was too slow or too fast: If you're used to playing on a fast court, it can be difficult to adjust to a slow court, or vice versa. This can lead to unforced errors and frustration.

The balls were too bouncy or too flat: The quality of the tennis balls can also affect your play. If the balls are too bouncy, they can fly over the court. If they're too flat, they can die at the net.

I had a bad case of nerves: Even the best players get nervous sometimes. It's natural to feel some anxiety before a big match. If you're feeling nervous, it can be difficult to focus and play your best.

I was feeling under the weather: If you're sick or tired, it's going to be hard to play your best tennis. This is a legitimate excuse, but it's best to use it sparingly.

"You can't be serious!"

JOHN MCENROE
(INFAMOUS
OUTBURST)

Not Moving Feet Well: This excuse is perfect to use if you're not getting into position quickly enough or if you're not getting your feet under your shots. It shows that you're aware of the problem and that you're trying to fix it.

Not Hitting The Ball Deep Enough: This excuse is perfect to use if you're hitting too many short balls or if you're not hitting the ball with enough power. It shows that you're aware of the problem and that you're trying to make an adjustment.

Not Reading Opponent's Serve: This excuse is perfect to use if you're struggling to return your opponent's serve. It shows that you're aware of the problem and that you're trying to focus better.

Not Hitting Volleys Well: This excuse is perfect to use if you're struggling to hit clean and consistent volleys. It shows that you're aware of the problem and that you're trying to improve your volleys.

Not Feeling Confident: This excuse is simple and straightforward, but it can be very effective. It shows that you're being honest and that you're not afraid to admit when you're not feeling your best.

Not Taking My Chances: This excuse is perfect to use if you're being too passive or defensive or if you're not going for your shots enough. It shows that you're aware of the problem and that you're trying to be more aggressive.

Not Making The Right Decisions: This excuse is great to use if you're making a lot of tactical mistakes or if you're not hitting the ball to the right places. It shows that you're aware of the problem and that you're trying to make better decisions.

Trouble With My Timing: This excuse can cover a wide range of problems from not being able to hit the ball cleanly, to missing returns or volleys.

Not Playing With Enough Patience: This excuse is perfect to use if you're rushing your shots or if you're not waiting for the right opportunity to hit.

"Tennis is a game where you
have to keep your head while
you lose your heart."

RAFAEL NADAL

Not Hitting The Ball With Enough Spin: This excuse can be used if your shots are not staying in the court, or if you're not getting enough power on your shots.

Too Many Unforced Errors: This is a general excuse that can be used to explain a poor performance. It's honest and it shows that you're aware of your mistakes.

Time Constraints: Some players claim they didn't have enough time to prepare or warm up properly, using this as an excuse for a lackluster performance. This excuse suggests that with more time, they would have performed better.

Not Playing Aggressively Enough: This excuse is perfect to use if you're playing too passively or defensively. It shows that you're aware of your playing style and that you're trying to make an adjustment.

Rapid Ball Movement: Swift tennis ball movements, can make it hard to control your shots and maintain accuracy, reducing your chances of winning rallies.

Racket Off Balance: Racket feels off-balance, throwing off your swing completely

Out Of Sync with Doubles Partner: Being unable to interrupt your playing partners reaction to situations causes confusions and mistakes

Unresponsive Tennis Balls: Playing with "dead" tennis balls causing a lack of reaction off the racket and a loss of speed.

Butterflies In Stomach: Butterflies in stomach causes a lack of focus and concentration during the game.

Playing Partner's Grunting: Playing partner's grunting is throwing off my rhythm.

Fashion Frustrations: Anything from new tennis shoes are too squeaky to Visor keeps slipping down blocking my view or headband is so tight, it's cutting off the circulation to my tennis brain!

"Is only a tennis match. At the end, that's life. There is a syndrome in sports called paralysis by analysis. The ideal attitude is to be physically loose and mentally tight."

ROD LAVER

CHAPTER 3: THE EXCUSES: A LITTLE MORE FAR FETCHED!

Sun Glare: "I couldn't see the ball clearly because of the blinding sun glare. It was like trying to play tennis on the surface of the sun!"

Overly Enthusiastic Court: "The court had way too much bounce. It felt like I was playing on a trampoline out there."

Sneaky Wind Gusts: "The wind was incredibly tricky today. It kept changing directions at the worst possible moment, making my shots unpredictable."

Sluggish Tennis Balls: "Those tennis balls must have been dead. It was like hitting a brick wall with my racket."

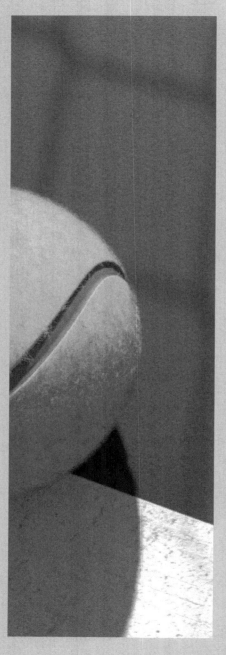

Bird Distraction: "I got distracted by a noisy bird on the court. It was like a feathered cheerleader with perfect timing for its squawks."

Allergy Attack: "My allergies suddenly kicked in during the match. Sneezing and serving don't mix well."

Lost Tennis Grip: "My grip started slipping mid-rally. I had to play the last few points with a racket that had suddenly turned into a bar of soap."

Mysterious Court Divot: "There was an unexplainable divot in the court that made me trip at the worst moment. I think it's the tennis court gnomes at work again."

Butterfly Attack: "A butterfly flew into my face just as I was about to smash a winner. I couldn't decide whether to swat it away or go for the shot."

Tennis Ball Rebellion: "The tennis balls staged a revolt against me. They started doing unexpected bounces, as if they were plotting a coup."

Psychic Opponent: "My opponent must be psychic. They always seemed to know where I was going to hit the ball before I did."

Inexplicable Fog: "A sudden and inexplicable fog rolled in, turning the court into a scene from a spooky tennis movie. I couldn't see a thing."

"You have to believe in yourself when no one else does. That makes you a winner right there."

VENUS WILLIAMS

Phantom Tennis Ball Thief: "My tennis balls disappeared one by one. I suspect there's a tennis ball kleptomaniac on the loose."

Racket Personality Disorder: "My racket suffered from a sudden case of multiple personality disorder. It couldn't decide whether it wanted to be a forehand or a backhand racket."

Tennis Ball Rebellion, Part II: "The tennis balls formed a union and went on strike, refusing to bounce properly. I had to negotiate with them between points."

Supercharged Opponent: "My opponent had some kind of energy drink before the match. They were like the Flash on the court today."

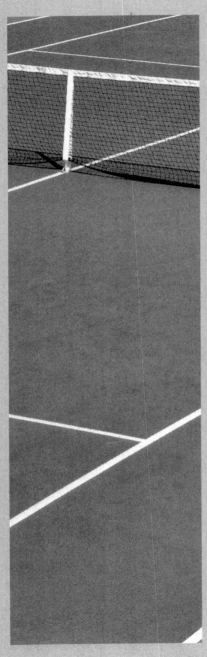

Phantom Net Height: "The net seemed to be higher on my side of the court. I couldn't get my shots over it no matter how hard I tried."

Butterfly Effect: "The butterfly flapped its wings in Brazil, and I double-faulted in frustration here. Chaos theory in action, I tell you!"

Shoe Malfunction: "My shoelaces rebelled mid-match, and I had to play the last set with one shoe untied. It was a guerrilla shoelace uprising."

Inexplicable Tennis Ball Magnetism: "The tennis balls had a magnetic attraction to the net. Every shot I hit seemed to gravitate toward it."

Tennis Ball Conspiracy:
"I suspect a conspiracy involving the tennis balls. They all seemed to be filled with helium today, floating just out of reach."

Mischievous Ball Kids: "The ball kids were playing tricks on me, swapping my racket for a banana at changeovers. I didn't notice until it was too late."

Sneezing Fit: "I had an unexpected sneezing fit during a crucial point. It's hard to focus when you're trying to serve and sneeze at the same time."

Devious Ball Machine: "The ball machine malfunctioned and started firing balls in random directions, as if it had developed a sense of humor."

"There is no way around hard work. Embrace it. You have to put in the hours because there's always something which you can improve."

ROGER FEDERER

Gravity Shift: "I think gravity shifted at the worst possible moment. My drop shots turned into moonshots, and my lobs barely left the ground."

Telepathic Umpire: "The umpire seemed to read my mind. Every time I thought of challenging a call, they'd announce the score without me saying a word."

Bermuda Triangle Ball: "One of my serves disappeared into a Bermuda Triangle-like vortex on the court. I hope it's having a nice vacation somewhere."

Pigeon Takeover: "A squadron of pigeons decided to stage a takeover of the court during my match. They were quite territorial about the baseline."

Tennis Ball Whisperer: "My opponent had a tennis ball whisperer in the stands who was sending telepathic instructions to the balls. No wonder they always seemed to land in!"

Ballerina Ball Bounces: "The tennis balls must have taken ballet lessons. They were executing perfect pirouettes and arabesques before landing."

Time-Traveling Opponent: "My opponent must have had a time machine. They were at the net and the baseline simultaneously, returning every shot with ease."

Sudden Ball Inflation: "The tennis balls seemed to inflate spontaneously during the match. It was like playing with miniature beach balls."

Court-Side Construction: "They were doing construction work right next to the court, and I think a jackhammer might have accidentally shaken up my backhand."

Sudden Rain of Tennis Balls: "Out of nowhere, it started raining tennis balls on the court. I tried to dodge them, but it felt like a tennis ball meteor shower."

Ghostly Ball Kids: "The ball kids were replaced by mischievous ghosts who kept hiding the tennis balls. It was like playing a supernatural game of hide-and-seek."

Sudden Shoe Swap: "My shoes spontaneously switched feet mid-match. I didn't notice until I started moving in circles."

"The mark of great sportsmen is not how good they are at their best, but how good they are at their worst."

MARTINA NAVRATILOVA

Tennis Ball Hypnosis: "The tennis balls had hypnotic powers. I couldn't take my eyes off them, and my footwork turned into a tennis waltz."

Instant Court Relocation: "I swear the court moved during the match. It was in one place for my serves and another for my volleys. I demand a GPS for tennis courts!"

Time-Traveling Tennis Ball: "One of the tennis balls seemed to have its own time machine. It would warp into the future, causing me to hit where the ball used to be."

Umpire's Sweet Tooth: "The umpire seemed to be indulging in candy during the match. Every time I hit the ball, they'd announce, 'Mmm, that's a sweet shot!'"

Holographic Tennis Ball Mirage: "A holographic mirage of tennis balls appeared on the court, making it impossible to distinguish real balls from illusions."

Tennis Ball Eclipse: "A rare tennis ball eclipse occurred just as I was serving. It was like trying to hit a moving shadow."

Time-Traveling Tennis Shoes: "My tennis shoes experienced a temporal glitch. One shoe was in the past while the other was in the future, making it a balancing act."

Overenthusiastic Fan Cheers: "One overly enthusiastic fan kept yelling 'Bravo!' every time I hit the ball. I couldn't focus with my own personal cheerleader."

Umpire's Lucky Coin: "The umpire had a lucky coin that they kept flipping before every call. It seemed to land 'out' whenever I was serving."

Court-Side Wind Tunnel: "I'm convinced there was a wind tunnel right beside the court. The ball would suddenly change direction mid-flight, like it had a mind of its own."

Tennis Ball Mirage: "A mirage of tennis balls appeared on the court, making me question which ball to hit. It was like playing tennis in a desert."

Umpire's Lucky Charm: "The umpire had a lucky charm necklace, and they'd rub it every time I was about to serve. Apparently, it worked like a charm for my opponent."

"The serve is the most important shot in tennis, and it's a lot like life. You get more than one chance to get it right, but you have to keep trying, and you have to concentrate."

SERENA WILLIAMS

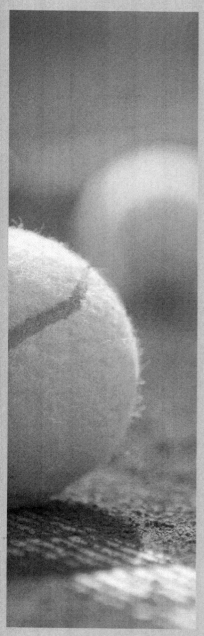

Tennis Ball Euphoria:
"The tennis balls experienced a euphoric state, bouncing higher with each hit. It was like they were on a trampoline."

Tennis Ball Jugglers:
"The tennis balls turned into expert jugglers, bouncing and juggling themselves mid-air. It was like playing tennis at the circus."

Tennis Court Illusionist:
"The tennis court employed illusionist tactics. The baseline seemed farther away when I was serving, and the net closer during volleys."

Tennis Ball Invisibility Cloak: "The tennis balls borrowed Harry Potter's invisibility cloak. I couldn't see them until they bounced off my racket."

Tennis Court Slide: "The tennis court turned into an ice rink, causing players to slide around like they were in a game of tennis curling."

Tennis Ball Glitch: "The tennis balls glitched like video game characters. They'd freeze mid-air or teleport to random spots on the court."

Tennis Ball Whack-a-Mole: "The tennis balls played a game of whack-a-mole with me. They'd pop up unexpectedly from different spots on the court."

Umpire's Lucky Coin Flip, Part II: "The umpire introduced a two-headed coin that always landed in my opponent's favor. It was a coin of perpetual luck."

CHAPTER 4:
A FEW TENNIS JOKES

Why did the tennis player bring a ladder to the match?
Because he wanted to reach new heights in his game!

Why do tennis players never get married?
Because love means nothing to them!

How do tennis players stay cool during a match?
They stand near the fans!

Why did the tennis player bring string to the match?
In case he needed to tie the score!

What do you call a group of musical tennis players?
The Racquettes!

Why do tennis players have low self esteem?
Because they have so many faults.

Why was the tennis player so good at baking?
He knew how to serve a perfect "slice"!

Why was the tennis court so loud?
Because the players raised a "racket!"

Why did the tennis player bring a suitcase to the match?
Because he wanted to pack a powerful serve!

What do you call a tennis player who doesn't let anyone else play?
A racketeer!

Why did the tennis player go to the bank?
To get his serve checked!

Why should dog owners invest in tennis balls?
They have a high rate of return.

Why did the man buy 9 racquets?
Because tennis too many.

My friend said to me, "We need to get to the tennis court before it opens."
I asked, "Why so early?"
They said, "It's first come first serve."

I had an opponent that wasn't happy with my serve.
They kept returning it!

I've heard they've made a website for depressed tennis players.
The problem is the servers are always down.

I asked my friend if they wanted a game of quiet tennis?
They replied what's quiet tennis?
It's just like regular tennis but without the racket.

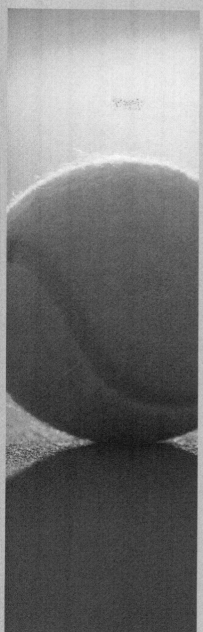

Whens the best time for playing Tennis?
Around tenn-ish.

I recently had an argument with my partner, and now their leaving me. They said I had an obsession with tennis and I'm too old. I said, "I'm only 40 love."

I got arrested for crying after losing my tennis match.
I've been charged with racket tearing.

What do you call a woman standing in the middle of a tennis court?
Annette.

A tennis ball walks into a bar.....
Barman asks: are you being served?

What did the tennis player say when they couldn't find their racket? "I'm really losing my grip!"

While out walking i bumped into a man walking his dog, he told me his dog was able to retrieve a tennis ball that landed 2 miles away
Sounds far fetched!

How do you always get severed at a bar straight away?
Go dressed as a tennis ball.

I was at my local Tennis club recently and I noticed someone playing naked apart from their shoes, I asked them what they were doing and they pointed to a sign. It said "Tennis Shoes Only"

"I fear no one, but respect
everyone."

ROGER FEDERER

CHAPTER 5:
TENNIS
FACTS &
STATS

Tennis is believed to have originated in the monastic cloisters in northern France in the 12th century

Tennis is known for its long history, making it one of the oldest sports still played today.

The modern version of tennis was developed in England during the 19th century.

Tennis balls were originally white, but they changed to yellow in the 1980s for better visibility on television.

Tennis is a popular sport worldwide, with approximately 17.68 million participants in the United States alone in 2017

The fastest recorded serve in men's tennis was 163.7 mph (263.4 km/h) by Samuel Groth.

The fastest recorded serve in women's tennis was 136.7 mph (220 km/h) by Georgina Garcia Perez

The longest tennis match in history lasted 11 hours and 5 minutes, played over three days at Wimbledon in 2010.

Martina Navratilova holds the record for the most singles titles won in tennis history, with 167 titles.

Novak Djokovic has the most Grand Slam titles in the Open Era, with 24 titles.

In 1973, Billie Jean King played against Bobby Riggs in a match famously known as the "Battle of the Sexes." King won, solidifying the role of women in professional tennis.

Steffi Graf is the only player to achieve the Golden Slam, winning all four Grand Slam titles and an Olympic gold medal in a single year (1988).

rtina Hingis became the youngest Grand Slam champion in history when she won the Australian Open doubles title at the age of 15.

Tennis legend Roger Federer holds the record for the most weeks spent as the world No. 1 in the ATP rankings, with a total of 310 weeks.

The Guinness World Record for the longest rally is an astonishing 51,283 shots in 2017. The attempt took over 12 hours to complete!

The longest winning streak in professional tennis belongs to Martina Navratilova, who won 74 consecutive matches in 1984.

Highest-earning tennis players as of 2023:

Novak Djokovic $38.4 million
Serena Williams $19 million
Naomi Osaka $17.5 million
Roger Federer $16 million
Rafael Nadal $14 million
Ashleigh Barty $13 million
Bianca Andreescu $11 million
Dominic Thiem $10 million
Simona Halep $9 million
Daniil Medvedev $8.5 million

Please note that these figures represent estimated earnings before taxes and agents' fees. Tennis players earn income from various sources, including prize money, endorsements, and appearance fees.

The all-time career earnings of top tennis players are as follows:

Novak Djokovic: $175,281,484
Rafael Nadal: $134,640,719
Roger Federer: $130,594,33
Andy Murray: $64,123,366

These figures represent the total career prize money earnings for these players in their respective careers. Novak Djokovic currently holds the top spot with the highest career earnings in tennis

"You can't measure success if you have never failed."

STEFFI GRAF

As we reach the end of "The Little Book of Tennis Excuses," we trust that you've enjoyed this collection as a reminder that tennis is more than just winning matches. It's about the camaraderie on the court, the laughter shared with fellow players, and the enduring memories created long after the racquets have been stowed.

While the excuses you've explored within these pages may have brought a smile to your face, let's not overlook that tennis is a journey of continuous growth and exploration. Every match offers a chance to deepen our grasp of the game and enhance our skills. Sometimes, a missed shot can be a humbling lesson, underscoring that tennis, like life itself, is filled with mysteries, and true mastery takes time and dedication.

So, the next time you find yourself with a less-than-perfect serve or an unexpected double fault, remember that tennis isn't solely about the score but the entire experience—the thrill of the rally, the beauty of the court, and the simple joy of connecting with the sport. And if, in those moments, you discover yourself crafting a witty excuse or sharing a chuckle with fellow players, embrace it as a part of the rich tapestry that makes tennis such an extraordinary pursuit.

"The Little Book of Tennis Excuses" encourages us to find humor in our tennis adventures and to cherish the journey as much as the victory. It underscores that even when the win seems elusive, the memories we forge and the bonds we create are what truly matter.

As you close this book, we hope it leaves you with a grin on your face and a renewed enthusiasm for your next match. Remember, tennis is an expedition full of surprises, and the perfect excuse is just one swing away. Here's to lively rallies, memorable volleys, and a treasury of anecdotes to share for years to come.

"The moment of victory
is much too short to
live for that and
nothing else."

MARTINA NAVRATILOVA

Printed in Great Britain
by Amazon